101

Things to Make and Do with
Googly Eyes

Getting Started with
Googly Eyes

What is a googly eye?

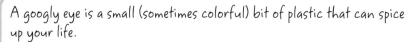

A googly eye is a small (sometimes colorful) bit of plastic that can spice up your life.

Seriously.

With a couple of googly eyes, you can turn rocks into pets, plain sunglasses into fashion statements, and desk stuff into newfound friends.

How would these magical feats be accomplished, you might ask?

Well, it's simple, really. Within these pages are 101 things to make and do with these amazing googly eyes, including games to play, crafts to create, and silly puns to make your friends giggle.

And when you're done with those 101 ideas, chances are you'll come up with 101 more of your own. The possibilities are endless!

Are you ready to tame the googly beast? To begin the googly journey?

Great! Let's get started.

First stop: your local craft store!

There are 101 ideas here, and each one uses different materials. Craft glue, felt, pom-poms . . . you name it, it's probably used in this book. However, anything you do with googly eyes is going to require one very important tool: your imagination! You don't have to go crazy buying stuff to use with googly eyes, as you will probably already have a lot of crafting materials at home!

Don't keep the googly fun all to yourself.

Have googly-eyed get-togethers with your friends, or invite your parents to join in on the fun (especially if something seems hard to do on your own).

Above all, have fun!

1 Create an "Eyesore"

Q: What's an eyesore?

A: An eyesore is something that looks out of place, like a scar or a blemish.

Make your own!

Create your own eyesore by gluing googly eyes to a bandage.

2 Give Your Eye Teeth . . .

. . . to the tooth fairy!

Glue googly eyes to a patch or a small piece of patterned fabric and attach it to a pillow. Next time you lose a tooth, stash it in there for the tooth fairy to find!

3 Potted Plants with Personality

The plants have eyes!

Glue a pair of eyes to your favorite pot, and then use paint or markers to create a funny face. Finish it off by using the plant for "hair."

4 Paper Clip Pals

Q: How can I give my homework some extra pizzazz?

A: Create a paper clip buddy to give your reports some personality!

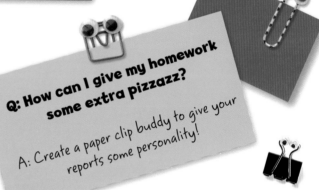

5 Rolling Eyes Pinwheel

Q: Why do people roll their eyes?
A: They're looking for something in the back of their brains.

Roll four eyes at the same time!
Glue an eye to each point of a pinwheel.
Now just wait for a good breeze!

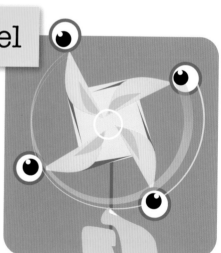

6 Picture This!

Display your favorite pix!

Craft a funky cat, an outrageous octopus, or a creepy-crawly spider to store notes and show off photos!

Supplies needed:

air-dry clay, plastic-coated paper clips (circle- or triangle-shaped), googly eyes

1

Roll the clay into a ball. Form or add clay details as desired.

2

Unroll the outer edge of a paper clip to create a straight end. Insert the straight end into the clay ball to make whiskers or legs.

3

Push googly eyes into the clay and let it dry.

7 Monstrously Menacing Door Hanger

Make 'em think twice before entering your room!

No one wants to enter a room full of monsters, do they? Add googly eyes and words of warning to a foam door hanger—and see how many intruders you can scare away!

8 Eye See the Light

Lighten up!

Give your light switch cover a real eye-opening addition—a pair of googlies!

Make your own!
These are sure to make your fancy feet a real shoe-in for the "Most Creative Dresser" award! Glue googly eyes, silk flowers, pom-poms, chenille stems, sequins, or anything else you like on your shoes to give them some real "face value."

'10 M'eye Mandala

Q: What's a mandala?

A: The word **mandala** means "circle" in the Sanskrit language (from India). Mandalas are symbolic patterns that are often made with a circle divided into sections. Traditionally, mandalas are created with colored sand, but you can also use markers, glitter glue, colored pencils, or even googly eyes!

Supplies needed:

paper, pencil, card stock, glue, colored sand, googly eyes

1
Draw a mandala design on paper. You can trace one from the opposite page or create your own.

2
Turn your design over and rub the back with a pencil.

3
Turn the design over and place it on top of the card stock. Trace over your design again.

4
The design is now on the card stock. Evenly apply glue to your design, one area at a time.

5
While the glue is still wet, apply colored sand to your design.

6
Allow the glue to dry and then shake off any excess sand. Now add some googly eyes!

Templates

11 Angel vs. Devil Salt & Pepper

Q: Why would I make these?

A: To make your food more heavenly or tempting!

12 Eye C U!

Magnetic Fun

Add eyes, beads, and some glitter glue to magnets to create funny faces.

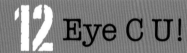

13 Eye Glass

Q; Why do I feel like I'm always being watched?

A: Because there are eyes all over your favorite drinking glass, silly!

Well, actually, it's a barrette.

But we won't tell anyone if you won't.

Make your own!

Take a regular barrette and add a pair of large googly eyes. For a furrier feel, add some faux feathers!

'15 Dotty Dominoes

Googly eyes make great polka dots, too!

Cut 28 pieces of craft foam into small rectangles. Draw a line across the middle of each piece. Add up to six googly eyes to each square and leave some squares empty. Each domino should be different. Now have fun playing!

15

❜16 Rest Your Wrists on This

Supplies needed:

fabric, scissors, glue, uncooked rice, felt, googly eyes

1
Cut two long oval-shaped pieces of fabric about the length of your keyboard.

2
Glue the fabric together, folding the edges under. Leave one end open and attach the tongue to the bottom layer.

3
Fill with rice and glue the opening closed. Glue on felt eyelashes and googly eyes.

'17 All Hands on Desk!

Q: My mom says someone should keep an eye on me. What does that mean?

A: Maybe you just need someone looking over you while you do your homework. How about some desk pals?

‘18 Perfect Pumpkins

Q: My pumpkin lacks personality. How can I give it some pizzazz?

A: Googly eyes make all the difference! Turn your pumpkin into a pretty princess or a punky pirate—just make it googly!

'19 Thumbprint Critters

Q: Help! I've got ink on my thumb. What do I do?

A: Get creative! Grab a pencil or pen and some googly eyes to make a crop of colorful critters.

20 Eye Spy

Q: My best friend is at my house, and we're bored. What's a new game we can play?

A: While your friend isn't watching, make an "Eye Spy" jar, filling it with a bunch of random stuff from your house. Make a list of everything you put in it.

Now show the jar to your friend for 15 seconds, then put it away. Ask your friend to write down everything she saw in the jar. Compare the two lists to see how many things she was able to remember.

The best part about this game? You can change the jar's contents after each game, so no two games are ever the same!

21 Eye'll Keep Your Place

Mark your spot!

With a little craft foam and some googly eyes, you can make a truly magnetic bookmark!

1

Cut a piece of foam 2 inches wide and 2 inches longer than the length of your book. Crease the foam 2 inches down from the top edge. Attach four small magnets as shown.

2

Decorate the flap with craft foam designs and googly eyes!

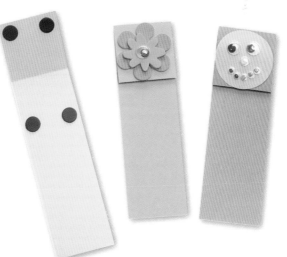

Opponent's
googly store

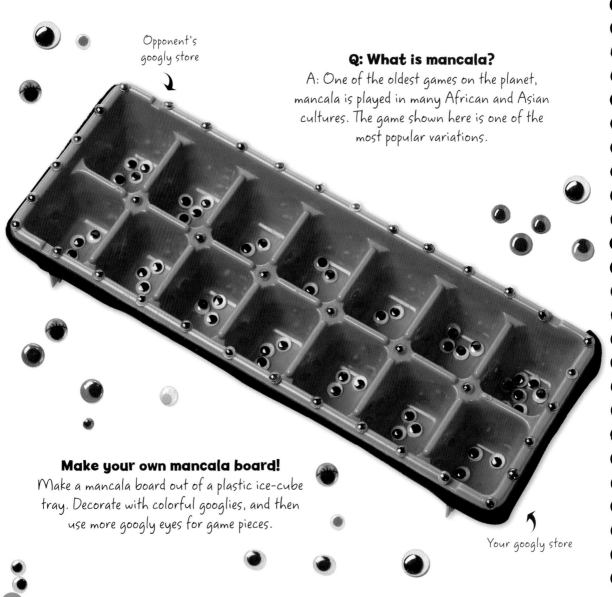

Q: What is mancala?

A: One of the oldest games on the planet, mancala is played in many African and Asian cultures. The game shown here is one of the most popular variations.

Make your own mancala board!

Make a mancala board out of a plastic ice-cube tray. Decorate with colorful googlies, and then use more googly eyes for game pieces.

Your googly store

The object of the game is simple: capture more googly eyes than your opponent!

1

At the start of the game, there should be three googly eyes n each hole. Each player also has a "store to the right of the board that holds captured googly eyes; the store is empty at the start of the game.

2

The first player starts by picking up all the googlies in one of the holes on her side of the board. Moving counterclockwise, she places one googly in each well until she s out of googlies.

3

While going around the board, if you run into your own store, deposit a googly. If you run into your opponent's store, skip it.

4

If the last googly you deposit is in your store, you get an extra turn. If the last googly you deposit is in an empty hole on your side of the board, you capture that googly and any googlies in the well directly opposite you.

5

Place all captured googlies in your store; it is now your opponent's turn. The game ends when one side of the board is empty; the player who still has googlies on her side at the end captures those pieces.

6

Count your googlies—the player with the most wins!

23 Butterflies with Eyes

It's a bird ... it's a plane ... it's a ... butterfly?

Give your googly eyes wings—and a clip, so they can sparkle anywhere!

Supplies needed:

craft wire, fabric, pencil, scissors, glue, small clothespins, googly eyes

1

Twist a 6-inch piece of wire into a sloping M shape, curving the end pieces back into the center to create wings.

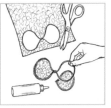

2

Wrap the end pieces into a tight coil in the center. Lay the wings on a piece of fabric, trace the outline, and cut the fabric to fit the wire. Glue the fabric to the wings.

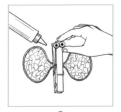

3

Glue the wings to the underside of the clothespin with the fabric pattern faceup. Glue googly eyes to the top of the clothespin and allow it to dry.

Here's another tip:
Add silky wings by cutting petals (two per wing) out of a silk flower and gluing them to the back of a clothespin.

Here's a tip:
You can also find a butterfly patch and glue on a clothespin and eyes.

24 All Eyes on Your Fingers & Toes

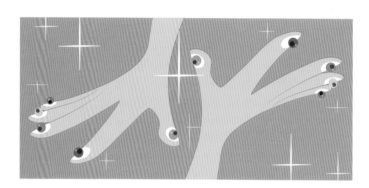

Get googly from hand to toe!

From fingertip to toenail, wow 'em with an "eye-deal" manicure or pedicure. Just use a bit of nail polish to attach an eye to each nail!

25 Eye Luv Flowers

Stash your glasses with style!

Glue googly eyes to self-adhesive craft foam flowers and decorate a plastic case for your glasses. Add rhinestones for extra sparkle!

26 Googly Glasses

Q: Why is everyone staring at me?
A: They're jealous of your new funky sunglasses.
What an eyeful!

27 Fishy Friends

Q: What do you call a fish with no eyes?

A: Fsh!

Supplies needed:

craft foam, scissors, glitter glue, two old CDs, glue, googly eyes, fishing line

1

Cut craft foam pieces for the tail. Add glitter glue to the tail and let dry. Cut one longer piece of foam for the fins and set aside.

2

With the tail sandwiched between the disks, glue the CDs together, with the colorful side out. Allow it to dry.

3

Push the fin piece through the hole in the center. Add googly eyes and heart-shaped lips. Loop string through the middle to hang.

28 Wand-ering Eye

Wish on a stick!

This wacky wand may not make your wishes
come true, but it will surely turn
all eyes on you!

Make your own!

Get crafty! Grab a plain
dowel rod and tie colorful
ribbons on the end. Finish it off
by gluing a huge googly eye on the top!

29 "X" Marks the Spot

Got a treasure to hide?
Decorate a shoe box with an old map,
a pirate flag, and a trail of googlies.
Stash yer treasure here, matey!

Magnetize your favorite photos.
Cut out the faces from your favorite goofy shots, add paper
clothes and bodies, and glue a magnet to the back.
Don't forget the googly eyes!

30 Eye'm Ready for My Close-Up

31 Rock on . . . **with your own pet rock band!**

1

Find at least three rocks that have flat bottoms
(so they can stand up straight).

2

Add googly eyes.

3

Use pipe cleaners, faux fur, or decorative trim to create rockin' hairstyles.
Don't forget to accessorize! Add piercings as desired.

For the microphone:
Coil a pipe cleaner at
the bottom and then twist up
the top to create a microphone.

For the guitar:
Use a pipe cleaner, a bottle cap, and glue to
craft a jammin' guitar!

For the drum set:
Glue bottle caps on top of pom-poms.
Cut pipe cleaners to create drumsticks,
and add a bead to the end of each.

32 Have You Seen My Ring?

Everyone will want a look at this jewelry!
Add an eye or two for a ring that
just screams "Look at me!"

33 Eye-rings

Q: What do you get when you wear googly eyes on your ears?
A: An earful of compliments!

Make your own!
Use craft glue to attach a pair of googly eyes to
earring backs (found in your local craft store).

Uninterrupted beauty rest!
With this clever craft, you'll still appear
wide awake to everyone else. But behind the
mask, you can take a blissful nap.
Now that's crafty!

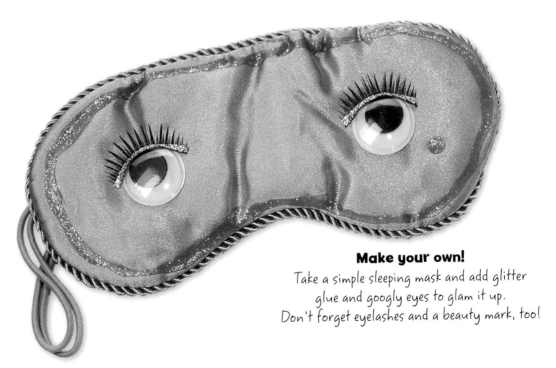

Make your own!
Take a simple sleeping mask and add glitter
glue and googly eyes to glam it up.
Don't forget eyelashes and a beauty mark, too!

35 Eye-full Tower

Ah, Paris, the city of love . . .
and home to the Eiffel Tower, where millions
of tourists go every year to gaze at
this amazing sight.
What's that, you say? You've never seen it?
Well, make your own!

Trace the template on this page
onto card stock. Then trim
it out and fill it with googly eyes.
Now you can gaze upon your
own "Eye-full" Tower!

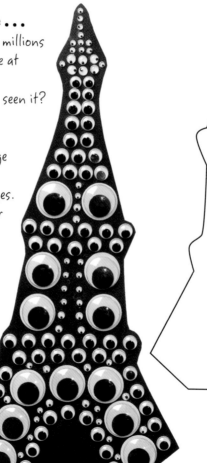

Template

36 Eye Found a Friend

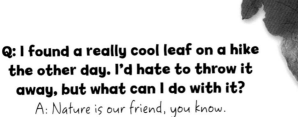

Q: I found a really cool leaf on a hike the other day. I'd hate to throw it away, but what can I do with it?

A: Nature is our friend, you know. Add googly eyes and turn your lost leaf into a natural companion!

37 Clothespin Art Critics

Give your latest masterpiece rave reviews!

Use googly eyes, clothespins, fabric, pipe cleaners, craft wire, and decorative trims to create these fancy clips—and then use them to hang up your favorite artwork! (Pay no attention if they roll their eyes—not everyone appreciates the classics!)

38 Tic-tac-eye

Jazz up this popular game!
Glue strips of funky fabric to card stock for the Xs, and glue large googlies to card stock for the Os. Let the games begin!

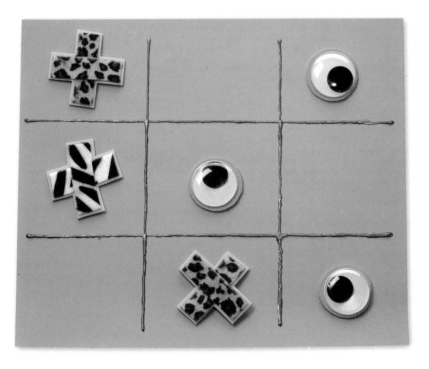

39 See This? It's a Gift!

Who needs boring gift wrap and a bow?
A googly-eyed gift is so much better.
Wrap a present in polka-dot paper, and then add
googly eyes to create a pretty package.

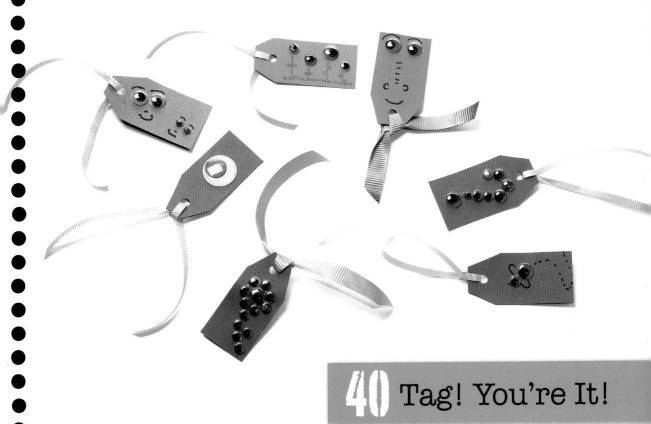

40 Tag! You're It!

Nothing says "It's from me" better than a googly gift tag!

Add eyes of all sizes and colors to make your own cool designs on gift tags.

Q: Whose face is that in the mirror?

A: It's yours, of course! But you can be sure you'll always have a happy reflection if you add a fun face to your mirror.

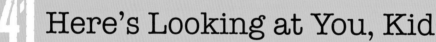

41 Here's Looking at You, Kid

42 Shake It, Don't Break It

Party like a googly!

Googly eyes make a great sound! Throw them in a toilet paper roll for an instant shaker, or use an old chip container—then when you're done you can use it to store your extra googlies!

Supplies needed:

decorative papers, scissors, toilet paper roll, glue, googly eyes, decorative trim

1

For fancy noisemakers, follow the template below to trace and cut out two paper circles. Cut slits at the dotted lines, and then bend the fringed ends down.

Template

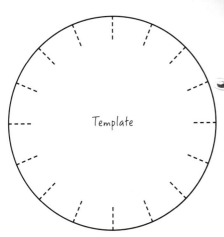

2

Glue one paper circle around one end of the toilet paper roll so that the fringed paper goes around the entire outside edge. Put googly eyes in the tube, then seal the other end with the other paper circle the same way.

3

Decorate the outside of the tube with colorful paper and trim. Don't forget to add googly eyes! Now make some noise!

43 A Key to the Problem

Q: Help! I lost my key. How can I find it?

A: Easy—you just need an extra pair of eyes!

Make your own!

You may never lose a key again—just add a colorful key cover
and a pair of googly eyes, and you'll never lose sight of it!

Q: My dad says he needs an extra pair of eyes to keep track of me. How can I help?

A: Attach a pair of googly eyes to a money clip or tie clip and present it to your dad. Problem solved!

45 Oooo . . . Look!

Draw attention to the matter.

To make this eye-catching magnet, glue two eyes to a magnetic strip, between an L and a K. Now the most important thing on your refrigerator is sure to get a look!

Q: What do you say when a balloon pops?
A: "May you rest in pieces!"

Balloons are people, too.
Well, maybe not, but you can make them look
like people if you add googly eyes and draw
some funny faces!

Supplies needed:

balloons, permanent markers,
googly eyes, glue, scissors,
craft foam, felt, ribbon

1

Blow up a balloon and tie it off. Draw
a face with a permanent marker.
Glue on googly eyes.

2

Cut a 10- x 2-inch strip of craft foam
and glue one end to the other to
make a ring. This will be the base
for your balloon.

3

Decorate the base with more foam,
felt, ribbon, or other decorations.
Set your balloon on the base
and display it with pride!

Q: Hey, what's a hedgehog?
A: Hedgehogs are spiny mammals that live in Asia, Africa, Europe, and New Zealand.

Q: So why would I want one on my desk?
A: This particular hedgehog makes a nice pencil holder, and he's kind of fun to look at, too.
Where's your sense of adventure?

47 Handy Hedgehog

Supplies needed:
air-dry clay in various colors, small glass bottle, pencils, googly eyes

1
Roll different colors of clay together to create a marbled effect.

2
Press clay around the bottle and shape into a ball. Add a piece of black clay for the nose, and four pieces for the feet.

3
Insert pencils into the clay to create holes for the "quills," but remove the pencils until the clay is dry.

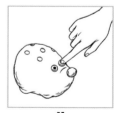

4
Press googly eyes firmly into the clay. Let dry completely before reinserting the pencils.

48 Critter Cap

Q: What's that on your head?

A: It's a creature you've crafted creatively for your cap . . . all it takes is a pair of googly eyes, a pom-pom, some glue, and a little glitter glue or faux feathers!

49 Pencil Pets

Make your own!
Glue a piece of faux marabou or
a pom-pom to the top of your pencil.
Add googly eyes and you've got
a new friend!

50 Eye for an Eye

Need something to keep your hair
out of your eyes?
Grab a clean pair of chopsticks and add googly eyes
to the ends. Just pull your hair back into a bun
and use your chopsticks to secure it in place. Voilà!

51 Egg-cellent Pals

Q: What do you call a mischievous egg?
A: A practical yolker!

Make your own!
Add googly eyes and other decorations to plastic eggs to create these fun and funky little containers.

52 Kissable Kritters

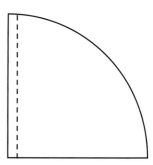

Template

Sweet treats with personality!

Trace the template above onto fabric or card stock. Then glue together the edges
and top a chocolate treat. Wait—don't forget the googly eyes!

Want a unique way to seal that note? Add some glitter glue and a pair of eyes!

53 My Eyes Are Glued to This Letter

Talkin' Turkey

Bet the pilgrims wished they had these!

These turkeys may not have been at the first Thanksgiving dinner, but they can be at yours!

Supplies needed:

pom-poms, glue, scissors, craft foam, googly eyes, feathers, card stock, stick-on letters

1

Glue two pom-poms together. Using the templates below, cut out the feet and beak from craft foam; glue them on.

2

Glue on googly eyes and feathers for the tail.

3

Fold a piece of card stock in thirds; glue at the bottom to create a tent. Glue a smaller piece of card stock to the front and then add your guests' names with stick-on letters.

Templates

55 B-Eye-N-G-O

Ready for an eye-popping game?
Use googly eyes as markers for your next bingo game!

B	I	N	G	O
21	16	4	15	30
11	8	1	28	29
19	27	FREE!	18	25
17	26	6	12	7
9	5	24	14	2

B	I	N	G	O
5	29	●	10	3
●	2	●	24	28
4	26	●	23	30
15	14	●	22	●
13	●	●	18	11

These socks are a sight for sore eyes!

Some socks already have goofy creatures on 'em—all you have to do is add googly eyes to make 'em even goofier!

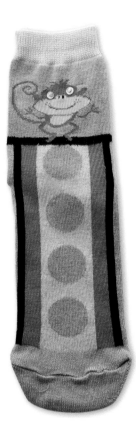

Hop to it!

56 Sock It to Me

Nothing says "winner" like a giant eye!
With these eye-catching award ribbons, you can reward anyone for a job well done!

57 Eye Win!

Supplies needed:
ribbon, scissors, glue, paper cupcake liners, googly eyes, stick-on letters

1
Cut two strips of ribbon to the desired length; glue to the back of a cupcake liner.

2
Glue a large googly eye to the front of the liner.

3
Press the letters onto the ribbon; trim ends of ribbon in an inverted V.

58 Watch This!

Make your own!
Use craft glue to attach googly eyes to a black watch band for timely fashion.

59 Have You Seen My Headband?

Q: I've heard people use the phrase "in my mind's eye." Does your mind really have an eye?

A: Well, not an actual eye like the kind that has eyelashes. But you can have an extra pair on your head if you glue some googly eyes to a headband!

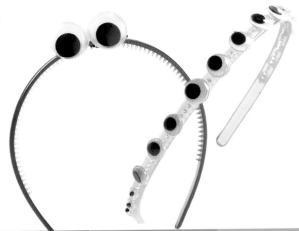

60 In the Blink of an Eye

Watch closely . . . while I make this eye disappear!

Keep a googly in your pocket. When there's a magic moment,
tuck it in your fist and, instead of pulling a quarter out from
behind someone's ear, surprise them by pulling out a googly eye!

61 Charming Cups

Make your own!

Take paper tags (found at office supply stores) and add a funny face. Add a split ring and poke through a plastic cup for a truly charming drink!

62 Super Sock Creature

Supplies needed:

knee-high sock, pillow stuffing, yarn, glue, foam flowers, scissors, chenille stems, pom-poms, googly eyes

1

Stuff the foot of the sock with pillow stuffing until firm. (The foot of the sock becomes your creature's head, and the toe of the sock will be its chin.)

4

Squish the stuffing around in the body until it's steady enough to stand. Glue two foam flowers to the base for feet.

2

Tie a knot around the neck with a piece of yarn. Fill the leg of the sock with more stuffing.

5

Glue foam flowers to two chenille stems for the hands. Glue the stems at the back of the body; glue one more flower over that to cover it.

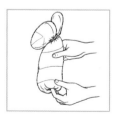

3

Tie a knot with another piece of yarn at the top of the sock to close it up. Now push the end of the sock up inside the body.

6

Add pom-poms and googly eyes for the face; use small foam flowers for eyelashes.

This friendly face is sure to cheer up any grump! With a few simple supplies, you can create your own sock buddy!

63 Takin' the Red Eye

**One direct flight,
coming your way!**

For a real red-eye flight, make a
paper airplane out of red paper;
add red eyes and let it fly!

64 Money Monster

**This creature eats
your money!**

Well, okay, he'll give it back if
you're nice. Just add eyes to
any coin purse to make your
own money monster!

65 Keep Your Eyes Peeled

It's definitely more fun to eat your veggies when they're smiling back at you! Just use tape to make faces on your food—felt smiles are optional!

66 Eye Need to Make a Call

Make your phone something to look at!
You can create a phone charm or decorate your phone with googlies—eye-ther way, it looks pretty crafty!

67 Lollipop Ghosts

Knock, knock.
Who's there?
Boo.
Boo who?
**Don't cry your eyes out—
here's a lollipop!**

Supplies needed:

pom-poms, craft glue, chenille stems, googly eyes, paper, scissors

Make your own!

All you need for this creepy-crawly creature is a couple of pom-poms, some chenille stems, and a pair of googly eyes. Glue a small pom-pom onto a large pom-pom. Bend and attach chenille stems and add some googly eyes.

68 Spooky Spider

Spin a web!

Just fold a square piece of paper in half to create a triangle and then fold it again to create a smaller triangle. Make several cuts following the long edge of the triangle. Round the corners to finish.

Origami Zoo

It's a whale of a craft!

Origami is the art of folded paper—
and with googly eyes, these origami
creatures really come to life!

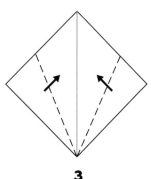

Whale folding instructions:

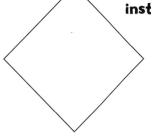

1
Start with a square sheet of colored paper.

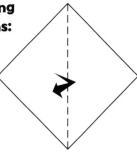

2
Fold the right point over to the left to make a center crease. Unfold.

3
Fold the lower right and lower left sides to meet at the center crease.

Make a zoo full of paper pals!

Check out an origami book from the library or look online for more origami animal ideas and patterns.

4

It looks like a kite. Now fold the top point down to meet the corners.

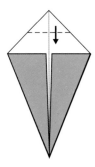

5

Fold the right side over the left along the center crease.

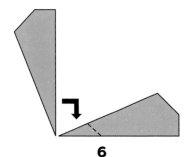

6

Turn 90 degrees and fold up the end point to make a tail. Add googlies!

70 Cross-Eyed Snapshots

Make your own!
Take your favorite photo, add
extra-large googly eyes, and frame!

Q: My cat won't eat his food. How can I get Fluffy excited about dinner?

A: Give your finicky feline something to cheer about—a food container with personality! Use craft foam to create a pet portrait, then add pom-poms, felt, and googly eyes!

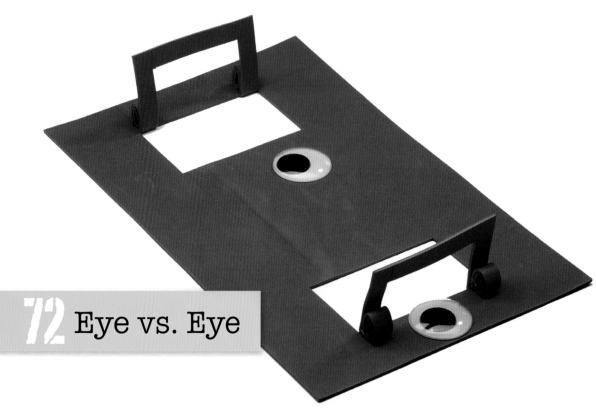

72 Eye vs. Eye

Can't see eye to eye with someone?
Forget your differences and play a game of table
hockey with googly eyes as the game pieces. You
can use posterboard or foam to make the playing
field and your fingers as the hockey sticks!

73 Rainy-Day Boots

Take the gloom out of a cloudy day!

Glue googly eyes, pom-poms, foam flowers, or even faux marabou to your galoshes and then go singin' in the rain!

This is no ordinary bracelet!
The googly eyes may look like unusual jewels at first glance, but look closer for a real eyeful!

74 More Than Meets the Eye

75 Flip & Flop

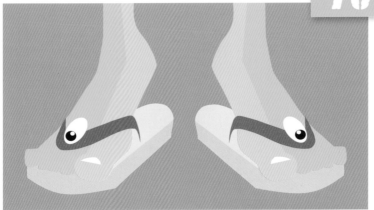

Q: How can I make my flip-flops more fun?
A: Add googly eyes, of course! Just one extra-large googly is all you need for each shoe. Then you'll be flip-flopping in style!

76 Flippin' Eye

Can't decide?

Flip an eye instead of a quarter—and don't forget to call eyes or tails!

77 Evil Eye Bracelet

Is someone staring you down?

Give 'em the evil eye right back. Attach one large and several small googlies to a wristband, and then flash it at anyone who dares to eyeball you.

78 Pillow Monsters

There's a monster on my bed!

There's nothing scary about these monstrously cute pillows! With a needle and thread, some felt, and a pair of googly eyes, you can make your own mini monsters, too.

Supplies needed:

paper, pencil, felt, embroidery thread, needle, pillow stuffing, googly eyes, fabric glue

1
Draw your own unique monster design on paper. Trace the shape of the monster on two layers of felt and cut them out.

2
Sew the pieces together, leaving a small section open. Fill with pillow stuffing, and then stitch up the hole.

3
Add googly eyes and felt features; secure with fabric glue.

Simple sewing tips:

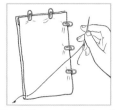

Getting started
Hold the two pieces of your design in place with paper clips. Thread the needle, knotting one end. Poke the needle between the two layers and pull through until the knot catches.

Stitching
Now push the needle through both layers close to the first stitch. Pull until there is a small loop. Stitch through the loop and pull tight to create a knot.

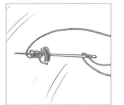

Knotting
To tie off, slip the needle through your last stitches. Wrap the thread around the needle and pull the needle through.

Make your own!
Plants get lonely, too. Make a friend
for yours with a plastic spoon and
some googly eyes.

79 Keep an Eye on My Plant

80 Beady-Eyed Bobbles

Need a fun desk pal?
Make a beady-eyed bobble—
it's sure to make you giggle!

Make your own!
Just use wooden beads, googly eyes, and coiled
craft wire to create your own bobble pal.
Add felt, foam, or feathers if you want!

81 Playful Puppets

Talk with your hands!

Start with a glove or a mitten, add googly eyes, felt, and yarn, and you've got a puppet parade!

82 Socked-In Snowmen

Q: It's July, but I miss wintertime and snowball fights. What can I do?

A: You can make sock snowmen any time of the year!

Supplies needed:

small white sock, uncooked rice, small rubber bands, glue, googly eyes, buttons or beads, ribbon, pom-poms, twigs or chenille stems, scissors

1

Pour rice into the sock and create body sections by wrapping rubber bands around the middle. Leave at least 1 inch at the top.

3

Glue on googly eyes and other details to create the nose, mouth, and buttons. Tie a ribbon around the neck for the scarf and top the hat with a pom-pom.

2

Secure a third rubber band around the top of the sock tightly; pull the top of the sock back down over the top to make a hat. Glue it in place.

4

Poke two small twigs or chenille stems into the middle section for the arms. (If the socks are thick, use your scissors to poke a hole through the material first.)

83 Googlies in the Snow

Q: What two letters did the snowman say once he got his eyes?
A: "I C!"

Make your own!
Try giving your next snowman googlies for eyes instead of coal!

84 Eye See Your Point

Do you get the point?
These colorful pushpins are made even cuter by
their googly-eyed decorations!

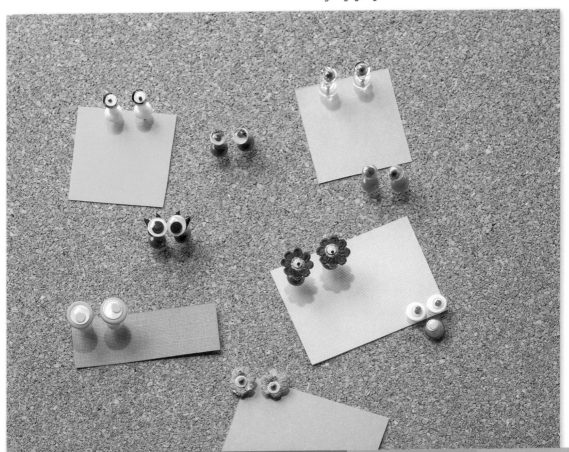

85 Colorful Butterfly

Did you know that a butterfly's eye is about 100 times less accurate than a human's?

So give this butterfly made of colorful craft sticks a handful of extra eyes— maybe it will help!

Before a butterfly grows up, it's a caterpillar . . .

Create your own caterpillar by twisting a green chenille stem and adding a pair of googly eyes!

86 Cute Caterpillar

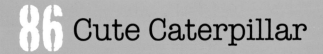

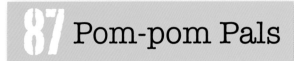

87 Pom-pom Pals

Make your own!
Alien? Monster? Harmless puffy friend?
The choice is yours!

88 Third Eye

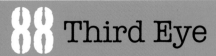

Are you a psychic?
Probably not, but you may be able to
convince your friends that you can predict
their futures with your amazing "third eye."
(Hey, just use tape to stick that thing
to your head!)

89 Bottle-Holder Buddies

Need someone to remind you to drink your water?

Create a googly-eyed bottle buddy to remind you to quench your thirst!

Supplies needed:

water bottle, thin and wide ribbon, craft glue, silk flower, pom-pom, googly eyes

1

Start by cutting a piece of thin ribbon that's long enough to go around your bottle and create a handle. Glue both ends to the bottom of the bottle.

2

Wrap thicker ribbon around the middle (over the thinner ribbon) and glue in place.

3

Glue on a silk flower, a pom-pom, and a pair of googly eyes to complete your bottle buddy.

90 Eye Candy

Q: What's a unique party favor to give out at my birthday party?
A: Something googly, of course!

Make your own!
Start with a plastic cup. For the pirate-worthy booty pictured here, add one googly eye, one patch, one felt mouth, and one strip of a bandanna. Add chenille stems for the patch strap and use two twisted together for the handle. Don't forget the loot!

You've heard of goose bumps, right?

Sometimes you get them when someone is staring at the back of your head. Maybe someone like . . . a cactus with eyes?

91 Prickly Stares

92 Eye, Matey

Are you the leader of your pack?
Show them who's captain—make like a
pirate and wear an eye patch! Arrgh!

93 Loaded Dice

Make your own!
Load up a pair of foam cubes with
googly eyes of all shapes and sizes!

**Spice up your lunch—
or your pooch's!**

A simple brown bag looks so much cuter
with some googly eyes and a little art!

Templates for doggie bag:

mouth

sides of face

tongue

face background

ears

nose

95 Keep It Eye-C

Q: Hey, have you seen my drink?
A: I think so—is it the one staring me in the face?

Make your own!
Add a rim of googly eyes to a drink cubby. Get out
a permanent marker and draw a tubby cubby pal,
and then give it a pair of googly eyes!

96 Eye-Love-You Card

Supplies needed:

card stock, pencil, scissors, black marker, glue,
googly eye, doll eyelashes, foam hearts,
rickrack trim, letter U sticker

1

Fold card stock in half. Draw an eye shape
on the front of the card and cut out. Trace edge
with black marker.

2

Glue eye in center of opening. Close
card and glue eyelashes to front.

3

Glue on foam hearts and rickrack trim;
apply the letter U sticker.

97 Private Eye Badge

Do you ever get asked for your "eye-D"?

Make your own private eye badge, complete with a
large googly eye, to prove to any doubters that you
are a real detective.

98 Pudgy Piggy

Stash your cash!
Start by finding a plain white clay piggy bank, paint it pink, and embellish with googly eyes. Then start saving!

99 Wacky Walker

Q: Can you walk like an Egyptian?
A: Even if you can't, this guy can!

Twist a chenille stem into a head and two legs, and then twist on an additional chenille stem for the arms and torso. Now make your flexible friend get funky!

₁₀₀ Bathroom Buddies

Make your own!

Everyone likes a friendly face first thing in the morning—and these bathroom buddies won't let you down!

Ever heard of a plant that keeps a watchful eye on you?

This one keeps a lot of eyes on you! Just add googlies to any silk plant for this eye-popping effect!

'101 Bloomin' Eyes

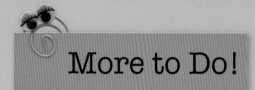

More to Do!

It's a googly world out there!
These are just 101 of the things you can make and do with googly eyes. What other ideas can you come up with? The possibilities are endless!

Silver Dolphin Books
An imprint of the Advantage Publishers Group
10350 Barnes Canyon Road, San Diego, CA 92121
www.silverdolphinbooks.com

ISBN-13: 978-1-59223-805-7
ISBN-10: 1-59223-805-X

Created by Walter Foster Publishing, Inc.
Creative Direction by Pauline Foster
Written by Samantha Chagollan
Illustrations by Adrian D'Alimonte
Instructional Illustrations by Diana Fisher
Photography by Steve Giraud
Art Direction by Laurie Young
Cover Design by Gary Martin
Production Design by Rae Siebels
Crafts by Heidi Kellenberger, Rae Siebels,
   Pam Thomson, Jenna Winterberg, Laurie Young
Production Management by Toni Gardner, Irene
   Chan, Lawrence Marquez, Nicole Szawlowski

Made in China.

1 2 3 4 5 11 10 09 08 07

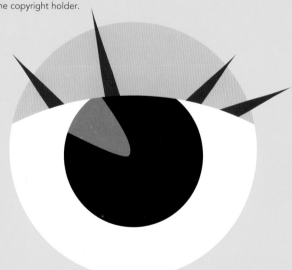